The Gift of Sirr

Secret Whispers Towards Inner Consciousness

Awaken to the melody calling you ...

Samineh I. Shaheem
JV Delalunas

GW00728045

iUniverse, Inc.

New York Lincoln Shanghai

The Gift of Sirr
Secret Whispers Towards Inner Consciousness

iUniverse books may be ordered through booksellers or by contacting:

iUniverse
2021 Pine Lake Road, Suite 100
Lincoln, NE 68512
www.iuniverse.com
1-800-Authors (1-800-288-4677)

Because of the dynamic nature of the Internet, any Web addresses or links contained in this book may have changed since publication and may no longer be valid.

The views expressed in this work are solely those of the author and do not necessarily reflect the views of the publisher, and the publisher hereby disclaims any responsibility for them.

Cover Design © 2007 by Arezoo Rezaei Afsah & Salma Shaheem.

Illustration collaborations by Salma Shaheem, Arezoo Rezaei Afsah, Samineh I. Shaheem, & JV Delalunas.

ISBN: 978-0-595-48209-2 (pbk)
ISBN: 978-0-595-60300-8 (ebk)

Printed in the United States of America

Contents

Acknowledgments

To all the people and energies we have come into contact with during this life, and all existences beyond time and place. May the threads woven inside this book echo eternal appreciation for the myriad of ways our lives intertwine and magically touch.

The Gift of Sirr is the work of forces beyond us, the writers/poets, and thus speaks to you of its own accord. Hear the messages within, as only you can, to understand things about the universe that lie beyond our writerly grasp. As you immerse yourself in each word, please allow those personal conversations between all our beings, to penetrate deep into your thoughts.

Initial Whispers

The Gift of Sirr—Secret Whispers Towards Inner Consciousness is a project that has been taking form for many years now. The initial foundation was laid when the right people crossed paths and began speaking about all that is profound and significant. Through life's stages, these eternal friends receive and recognize the divine honor of sharing the Sirr's essence. Thus, many masters and monsters played a pivotal role in inspiring the shape and character of this book. After many adventures, encounters and much exploration, we impart to you this gift; *The Gift of Sirr*.

Through different faiths, philosophies or schools of thought, some of you may already be familiar with the meaning of the word *Sirr*. However for those who have not been directly exposed to its origins, a brief introduction is necessary before the next step of this journey. *Sirr*, according to Sufi ideology, refers to things that are mysterious, 'a secret', and in Sufi symbolism, it is the centre of consciousness. By connecting to this feature of our soul, we are able to achieve union with our spiritual self in order to better understand concealed aspects of our being, the people around us and the purpose of our existence.

The collection of words that have been specially woven through this publication, is our humble attempt to try and hit such inner chords. We ask you to visit the messages of this gift in your own unique way. Some of you may wish to read the book cover to cover; others will randomly flip through the pages and poems; while still, there will be some who choose to be drawn toward a specific page and read the words intended for you in a particular moment. The method by which you orchestrate this process is irrelevant; what is important is that you have received the 'Gift' and can now welcome its presence into your spiritual world.

Fallen Angels

We heard you day and night
Pondering wrong and right,
Preparing for the fight.

When tears streamed down your face,
Questioning God's Embrace:
Angels Fell.

At times you lost in man's parade
Giving energy to his charade.
Participating in the race,
That asked you to forget your place.
Challenged again by plight,
You sometimes lost your sight—

And Angels fell when you cried.
But Angels rose when you died.

In darkness, you found light.

J.V.D

'When anger and harsh words are trying to poison your world, exile them and instead offer shelter to poetry and light.'

Invisible

I feel invisible, at times,
Even when here.
Should I twirl and twirl into the sky
So that I can once again appear?
And while I embark on this travel,
I may not desire to return
Because of all that I encounter, and unravel:
Joy, acceptance, passion,
Clarity and magic spells …
But I do return, time and time again.
'Why?' You ask, my curious friend.
So that I may share with you
All that I have discovered;
So that I may tempt your soul's mission
To be recovered.
Thank you, for inviting me back,
And putting my soul's purpose
Back on track.

S.I.S

'Truth reveals itself in many layers.'

Beautifully Captured

Love kidnapped me in a dream
And passed me around
Until I reached you.

You swallow me whole,
Inhale me with your kiss
And beckon me to come.

Oh, sweet precious love
Take me to your kingdom
And throw away the key.

J.V.D

'You already know this story.
You helped to author it.'

Healing

Take a seat and let's fill up the void,
Not only on the pillow,
But also of our passion destroyed.

Remind yourself of your childhood dreams;
Life is not just work, concrete, traffic and polluted streams.

Connect once again

To who you really wanted to be

And slowly begin to let go
Of the fake representation
Of everyone else's expectation of Thee.

S.I.S

'If you're asking this question, does it not mean that you need to communicate more openly? Ask the source.'

Sweet Sky

Sweet Sky, bring me closer;
Weave me into your life
And invite me inside—
To experience You.

Sweet Sky, bring me closer;
Lead me to your world
And we'll dance in the depths—
To all that is Love's Love.

J.V.D

'Each new encounter is a dream yet unexplored, a doorway to another world and a journey to unfold.'

Birthday

The day of birth is filled with mystery,
For it is the moment
We begin living our history.

And each year we are reminded
Of this great mission called life,

Visit this day of birth, as I know you will,
With harmony and not strife:

To make sure you always look back
At all your adventures
With joy and acquired wisdom,
So that you can continue living

A cherished life.

S.I.S

'You are not listening to the whispers.
Pay closer attention.'

Beyond Dunes

The desert is quiet
For those that can not hear—
But, in truth, she sings.

At day, the sun watches;
And at night, stars visit.
Time stops and listens:

"Oh Dearest Beloved—
Now I become the winds
And carry myself to you …

"Lift me beyond mountains;
Send me a boat at sea;
Tell me our love is true …"

The desert is quiet,
For those that can not hear
But, in truth, she sings.

J.V.D

'When you can not sleep, it is because Love is beckoning you to stay Awake.'

Fly

Butterfly butterfly,
I adore you so.

Not just today,
But from the first time you came to see me, so long ago.

Many have tried to understand
The patterns and designs of what you are;
So many assumptions, theories and declarations attached to you,
My superstar.

But don't be offended
By our misinterpretation and false illusions.
You know more than any other creature
That we are simply trying to metamorphosis
Out of our dense confusion.

Flutter your wings and clear the air,
Not to create a tornado or a love affair,
But to dance
The way you were born to dance …

Because only you know
What you must chance
So you can forever remain true
To your destined stance.

S.I.S

'The cover of a book may not give us a complete indication of the content, however do be weary of a cover which warns us of the story which might unfold.'

Inside The Candle Stick

I am but a wick;
Once flickering with sparks,
Now immersed in flame.

The candle reshapes—
I Remain.

I am but a wick;
Warmed by fire's love—
Dancing with its heats …

For in our burning—
My Heart Beats.

Beautiful flame,
It is you that keeps me alive.
If we only have two options,
Is it not better to keep burning than to fade?

J.V.D

'Agony is a force, which pushes us toward heaven and into ecstasy.'

My Steps

I sometimes wonder how the world looks;
Is it simple, twisted or full of hidden hooks?
Do we think and see in a true light?
Or are we sometimes blinded
By the difficulties of our fight?

I lay here
On Earths green sheet of protection,
And look back at you
While I wonder about the connection.

Do you see me as I am?
Or do you choose to see just Aries the ram?
Take a few moments to think about,
Why it is we wear these lenses
Limiting a deeper or more accurate turn out.

The sky may be vaster than the green sea,
However don't forget there will be
A time when my steps will be measured
Larger than the rest of me.

S.I.S

*'Shall you find yourself
in a reoccurring situation,
try something new
and listen to the teacher.'*

The Unicorn and Butterfly

The Butterfly followed the Unicorn
Through many lands,
As she eventually accepted
To live lost in his hands.

'Don't worry my Butterfly,' he would say,
'We will be safe here, forever and a day.'

'I stopped worrying long ago, my love,'
She answered,
'For it is only within this passionate cage that I feel I can truly fly.'

What might become of the Unicorn and Butterfly, you ask?

They might have to wear their masks,

In order to satisfy their earthly tasks …

But underneath it all,
As they reside in their heavenly
Open-door cage—
After performing like expert actors
On a universal stage;

They return to one another,
Regardless of time, place or age.

S.I.S

'Die for the one who is at least willing to get sick for you; and die for love because it is the only thing that will resurrect you.'

1 Spell + 1 Wish = 2 Bliss

In the forest, she cast her spell
And there before us, appeared a well.
From eleven rocks in the ground
Grew a waterhole, big and round.

Simple and silver from the distance,
I kindly offered my assistance:
"Fill the cups, but not too full.
Make a wish and then we go."

Entrapped by beauty in the wood.
Above the stone top, we then stood.
And there inside the well we looked.
Deep in trance, deeply hooked.

Golden liquid filled the pool—
So shocked I froze, just like a fool.

She took my hands in her own,
Dipped them in the water throne …

"Love, all you need is to taste one drop
And all our suffering will be stopped."
She laced my lips with her wet gold
Preventing us from growing old.

In the forest, she cast her spell
My wish came true but I couldn't tell …

Time had stopped and there we remain—
Still in a moment, without the pain.

J.V.D

'Life is not a fairy tale;
but it is a secret Garden.'

Conversation

As he wakes up and faces the world,
He knows what he feels
Because of what she has told.

He looks around for a familiar sign,
And finds her scent lingering
Like a beautifully aged wine.

Who is this stranger who has become the closest twin?

What did he do to deserve this win?

Some things don't have clear answers.

Some events don't allow in the weak dancers,
To move to the beats of the heart …

For it is only the truly blessed
Who know how to love when apart—

And then once again revive their senses when ending the depart.
'Live for me,' she says,
As he declares his undying love,
For without his life
She would only be an unwinged dove.

'Are we meant to be?' He asks.
She whispers an answer without any masks:
'If we are not meant to be, my angel,
Than destiny would have set me free
On that first night
When our paths crossed once again.'

Both need not explain the ending
Of love's pain,
For without that pain
There would be no lessons learnt,
No rainbow stains or passion gained.

So wake up to the song of morning
As she sings her words of adoration
And remember to always be mesmerized, and embraced
By the power of love's fascination.

S.I.S

'Reason may not always lead to solution, therefore stop searching for 'why' and begin lifting yourself toward the sky.'

Time Travelers

We visit ourselves
In another time and place—
Do you see us there?
Can you recognize our face?

Two different bodies perhaps—
But still the same souls;
Let the truth unfold
By what the Beloved knows.

We visit ourselves
In another time and place—
Do you see us there?
Can you recognize our face?

J.V.D

'Understand and accept that we are all connected.
Your actions and decisions will impact others.'

Lover's Trial

I wonder what he's doing
As I imagine him in my arms.
Does he know where he is being taken
As I try and wrap him in my charm?

I miss his scent, his smile
And all that others don't see.
He looks at me in a way which reminds me,
Only he holds the key.

I gladly impart
With the golden instrument
Used to capture my heart
For it no longer belongs to me
And should remained locked
While we are apart.

I ask him for forgiveness
When love's anger whips a painful scar,
I ask him to remember me
Only as the creature that makes him smile.

Because if he does anything otherwise—
He will dim the nights stars …

And send both of us to the Gods
To face the ultimate lovers trial.

And you know what they will say to us as we arrive
In front of justice's blind gaze?

'Don't be foolish young blessed lovers
By ruining your most beautiful days.'

So listen to them we shall my love
And a dove you will always be to me;
Even when love makes us sometimes feel unworthy
and lost in a vast dark sea.

Because you know in that sea,
I will finally find you and once again
Rekindle our candle lights hue.

S.I.S

'In the world of the Divine, there are no mistakes—only lessons to be learned.'

Messenger

Fill the hands, across the lands
And remind them of our art.
Mirror in eyes; all our tries,
Make an offering to the heart.

Cross the paths, but not for lasts—
Keep faith that we're together;
Bless our travels, while life unravels
And thank the Golden Feather.

J.V.D

'Look beyond the surface.
To some, dirt is nothing more than brown silt—but
it is also the soil nourishing seeds; and clay
shaping growth.'

Missing Twin

Where did you come from?
Where have you been?
I've looked for you like a missing twin.
I ask not because I doubt your perfection;
You have always been on the right track,
Searching for my reflection.

There was no better time than now.
There was no better place than here.

So take my hand in yours, as I make a vow
To join you, my dear,
On this sometimes wonderful and sometimes challenging
Frontier.

Together we will invite laughter and joy to accompany us.

But not fear, the occasional sadness, tears or fuss.

Not just a confidant partner or a lover,
But you to me,
Are my true other—

And an endless sea wanting to be discovered.

Accept my presence by your side;
For this is one knot that will not want to easily untie.

S.I.S

'The path to Enlightenment begins with the journey toward the Light Within.'

Beloved, I Am ...

Beloved, I Am Yours.
Wrap Your Wings Around Me,
Unlock the Golden Doors ...

Share With Me Your Sweet Warmth
Of Paradise Within—
And I Will Kiss the Light
That Glistens on Your Skin.

Beloved, I Am Yours.
Wrap Your Wings Around Me,
Unlock the Golden Doors ...

Guide Me to the White Dove
Singing Her Song of Calm—
And I Will Be the Streams
That Flow Between Your Palms.

Beloved, I Am Yours.
Wrap Your Wings Around Me,
Unlock the Golden Doors ...

Hold Me Close, My Angel—
Our Spirits Dance as One;
Be the Love That Ripples
Into the Burning Sun.

Beloved, I Am Yours ...

J.V.D

'Don't stop dancing just because a storm comes — let the rains renew your vigor and dance as if you were thunder itself.'

Experience

Suddenly we look back and wonder,
How much we were affected
By the experienced thunder.

So many years have passed …
Some felt slow, while others fast.

We know there was much more
Which we could have said and done,
So much more we could have learnt.

But don't focus on those moments,
One by one
—

Instead, weave together the lessons learnt like a fine silk thread.
Allow the final days of this passage
To pave the way,

For the arrival of your brightly flower filled future of a bouquet.

S.I.S

'Remember what is delayed may not be denied.'

Sweetness

Passion invokes me and I become fire—
Red love burning, inflaming with desire …
Rooms sweat with our bodies' scented oils;
Hearts pound, while the imagination boils.
High vibrations form between us,
On and on
Finely connected, no one can break the bond.

Many try to uncover such pleasing sounds—
But only you strike the cord,
Beyond all bounds.

Passion invokes me and I become fire—
Red love burning, inflaming with desire …
Champagne streams down the skin
And bodies cool;
Ready for berries in a hot chocolate pool.

The whole scene tastes like candy,
Made for two—
But the only sweetness here,
Is that of you.

J.V.D

'Paradise is a state of being where mind, body and soul unite.'

Seasons

Who are you to me? Shall I wait and see?
Or are the answers already growing
Out of our love tree …
There may be times
When the cold winter steals our warmth and affection
During those days,
I secretly tremble with anticipation.
But the spring slowly promises—

The rebirth of our destined selection …
When we are once again covered in elation.

The summer brings with it
Both heat and passion;
And if not too careful,
The Beloved may burn,
Losing her compassion.
Gladly, the fall we once again welcome;
For if it wasn't for the constant visiting
Of the seasons—
We would struggle to remember
That love has many reasons.

S.I.S

'You have been given the Gift of Choice.'

Love's Love

Laying on a bed of flowers
With our head facing upward,
Looking into the Sky's eye,
We open the door to our heart—
Letting go of all which resides inside:

Out pours feelings of serene sacrifice
Accompanied by crystal tears
Of a rare and combined feeling
Expressing deep joy and sorrow together—
From the depths of 'I Am' …

Love's love flying high
With wings of forgiveness,
Weaving trails in and out
With colorful light sparks,
Birthing Earth's child, Paradise.

Hear us birds sing,
For that too is our mourning—
And Morning,
By which the sun shall rise anew;
When all has flown
From the nest in our chest,
Relocating across the land,
Reuniting at Dawn,
Rejuvenating one will, one intent.
We will not close the door—

The latch that enables lock bursts away
By divine force of the glowing tree—

Once a planted seed within,
Now springing from our heart,
The true passage:

Rooting us—to Us, and We, to 'I Am'.
Standing firm with a thick trunk
Of unconditional love …

Spreading our branches,
Full of blossoming wonders—

Each twig offering gifts,
Different but similar—

From maturing orchids
To giving hands;
Fountains to rainbow extensions

Reaching into the sky …
While stardust rains upon us
With Dawn's Renewal
Cleansing the Circling Infinity
Of our being, Love's Love.

J.V.D

'When you seek justice, first think about how just you have been.'

Midnight Memories

Our lives ask us to awake
As each night our rhythm grows;
Revealing to us the fate
By which our movements flow.

Close your eyes sleeping beauty
And dance into my world;
Put your arms around my neck—
Step in close, as we twirl.

We bask beneath mango trees;
We lay in each other's arms;
We watch marmalade sunsets;
And share in endless charms.

Our lives ask us to awake
As each night our rhythm grows;
Revealing to us the fate
By which our movement flows.

Sometimes we enjoy silence;
Starring deep into our soul—
Our eyes speak with our body,
Remembering what we know:

We speak, laugh, whisper and cry …
Sing, make music and whirl;

We walk, swim, make love and fly—
Enchanted with a swirl.

Our lives ask us to awake
As each night our rhythm grows
Revealing to us the fate
By which our movements flow.

J.V.D

'In your heart, cherish those who are miles away—as much as those next to you. Distance disappears with love and understanding'

Lace

Breathless, as you envelop me
With your beautiful character.

Are you aware that it is you
That all those souls prefer?

Mesmerized,
Watching you sway with me
Through your attractive dance.

How enticing,
As you make sure you have exchanged
Many a glance.

I wonder about your composition,
Connected—
Yet made up of all these separate ambitions.

If you weren't 'Lace',
Tell me,
Would you choose to be a magician?

S.I.S

*'Beginning' and 'End' are two
of the same, born together.'*

Morning

Upon my wakening
The Earth was shaking
What once seemed real
I could not feel

Great walls crumbled
Grand men humbled
And there I stumbled

Into You.

J.V.D

'Don't be afraid to ask more questions. If things do not make sense, chances are, you are not looking at or being shown the full picture.'

Maybe

All that is gold may not shimmer,
All those who smile may not be so eager.

But have you also considered,
All that is quiet may not have withered,
Or all which seems to have lost its sweetness
May not always be bitter.

Wash your eyes of a false curtain,
And accept the Lover and Beloved
As eternal drinkers of the passion fountain.

S.I.S

'Those close to you have already answered this question, listen to them.'

Breathe

In and out; In and out—
Into each other …

Slow and Deep;
We Glow and Seep …

In and out; In and out—
Into each other.

Inhale Me;
Drink Me;
Expose Me
To Your Inner World …

Let us Dance,
Twist and Twirl—
And become intoxicated …

And then …

Exhale Me;
Slowly, Deeply;
Slowly, Deeply.

Divine Oxygen must be shared.

Give the world all within,
Take our spirits on a spin …

Breathe.

In and out; In and out—
Into each other …

Slow and Deep;
We Glow and Seep …

In and out; In and out—
Into each other.

Inhale Me.

Feel Me.

Pump Me

Through Your Body's Heart:

Let us Dance …
And never part—

Until we breathe no more.

… Breathe …

J.V.D

'Your Inner Candle burns with Bright Fire. Alight new flames from your wick. This Divine Element never dies — for when it seems to dim, it too is in the process of glowing.'

Dance

There are times when I need to dance.
If only you and all those who doubt my talents would
Give me a chance.
'There's no music playing,' you say.
'Those who need music don't understand what it means to
Dance,' I say.

Look at the arches and curves of my soul,
There is but little one can control.
Of course you may try—
Try and try, until I am ready to die.
For if I were to stop dancing,
I would surely see my life sadly whisk by.

S.I.S

'What a great plan —
Invite those hesitant to take a chance.'

Living Library

Between stacks of aged paper
And neatly shelved expressions,
Dusty surface asked to be cleared.

There stood Nietzsche and Satre,
Rumi and Aristotle—
Isles of books surrounding,
Waiting to be opened …

Eager to discover
What we would do,
When we found out:

They had been reading us—

Page by page, line by line,
Thorough and in-between,
Word by word not unheard …
Layer by layer,
Fiber by fiber—
Anticipating the Wake

J.V.D

'Ideas are realized through action — thought is nothing without Will. Intend to Do and Be.'

The Palace

The palace resembles me in many ways:
So many rooms, corners and angles on display.

How adventurous of you to have explored
All my dimensions—
Carefully analyzing each aspect
Of my characters hidden inventions.

You were tempted into my palace
For a reason.

What a fateful decision to ask you to remain with me
During life's different seasons.

However one facet I dare not take credit for,
And that is the way
In which through your presence
My palace has wonderfully altered,
For ever more.

S.I.S

'Short cuts may lead you to your destination sooner, however be prepared to leave many stones unturned.'

Mind over Matter

Surrounded by ocean in this emotion,
I cultivated my faith and devotion—
Believing in Miracles, Believing in Us.

At first appearance,
There was no way to you;
But experienced eyes trained me what to do.

So when the time was right,
I walked across water.

Believing in Miracles, Believing in Us.

J.V.D

'Do you understand? No man can test the hand of God—for when he does, he looses Faith. But if it were decided that be the mandatory stop on his journey—revealing to him new paths to an unequivocal power (and increasing his Faith 10fold down the road)—So Be It.'

You and I

I know I've seen you before;
It's been a few years.

I've seen you cry;
I've felt your tears,
Asking me why.
Know that you are always beside me,
Never apart.
Because what you and I have,
Has been written in the stars.

You may not see me now,
And it doesn't matter how,
But you and I were meant to be,
Like two reflections carved into a tree.

S.I.S

*'If the worst that can happen is a lesson learnt,
than imagine the best that might come out of this.'*

Magic Eyes

Magic Eyes, tell me what you see.
Magic Eyes, tell me what we'll be.

In the night you share your vision,
Sprinkling with insight
All that seems imprisoned.

Share with me not the pain and fears;
For what we have experienced
Pass years, let's save the tears.

Magic Eyes, tell me what you see.
Magic Eyes, tell me what we'll be.

At day you reflect to us, the Sun—
Illuminating pathways
Through which two become One …

Past, present and future are 'We'.
Share with me an adventure—
Together, we shall see.

J.V.D

'Intoxication is a powerful state,
Make sure when sober, you feel the same.'

The Kiss of Life

Raindrops tap dance on rooftop trees
In a forest hidden by poetry.
Seeping through the warm mist of yesterday
Are moonlit stars fluttering like butterflies.
Soft silky petals surrounding the meadows of

We

Gently stroke the secret life of bees
Painting blissfully wild emotions
With colors blended by fornicating flowers;
Seductively sweating a melodious dew of

Enchanted love songs.

Thunder roars with lions in the sky;

Earth tone vibrations ringing with each

"BOOM";

Fireworks ignited in the sacred eye;
Your hypnotizing kiss penetrating bolts of lightening;

Streaming inside and throughout the vessel

I Am;

Like a pink pool of pure sun radiating bright

With passion,

And dubbed with a rainbow trail of life's

Sweetness.

J.V.D

'When you are debating whether or not to pour out your soul, reflect upon your surroundings, and see that it is already everywhere.'

Mothers

To mothers and our mother's mothers.
You are the only thing closer to heaven's other.

I watch you as you cry alone at night,
Thinking that I am too young
To understand your plight.

And when you turn my way,
You wipe the tears away,
Pretending your wet eyes
Are only the reflection of the day.

Nothing I say or do will ever come close
To your sacrifice
Or advice.
But know that one day I will understand,
And an explanation I will command,
So that I can try to kiss away
Some of the irritating
And abrasive sand.

S.I.S

'A Moment is forever. Don't try and capture it—live and breathe it.'

When Stars Speak

When stars speak, the blue moon glistens;
Time stops in illumination
And the world stills to listen.

When stars speak, Lovers' sparkles show;
Oceans rise and pave paths
Beckoning One toward the soul.

How do I know?

So it goes, every time you speak to me.

J.V.D

'No need to count to seven before living your dreams.'

Moonlight

You are the relative of your daylight other.
Doesn't matter if you choose to be her sister, father or brother.
You need each other to light our worlds …

In the morning, afternoon, and evening,
In delightful twirls.

But my moonbeam,
A special shadow you cast.
Of all that is mysterious,
Profound and unsurpassed.

Through your silver pathway,
I find a world I thought I had lost.
Through your power,
I once again feel my emotions defrost.

For without you, I would feel incomplete.
And my midnight adventures
Would be tasteless and never so sweet.

S.I.S

'Don't let sweet memories from your past shackle you in a situation which is less than favorable. Those moments will not help with the turmoil of today or tomorrow.'

Almost There

The portals are open—
Escape the sands of time.
Leave doubt and anger,
And dance away with Rhyme.

Let the lands weep for you—
As have I ever long.
And meet me in the skies,
Where we can sing our song.

J.V.D

'Love finds you, even when you hide
and love will execute you,
to set you free.'

Stars

When the world sometimes feels
Concealed and quiet,

Don't look away …

It may be asking us to focus
On our internal riot—

For reflection
And not unnecessary inspection—

Which should guide us on a journey,
Worthy of selection.

Those dark and quiet moments
Might introduce important thoughts—
Suddenly in the same way
The north star would save young sailor's,
Not ready to be caught—
In the void of frustration
Engulfing us,
And trying to threaten,
Every conscious person's salvation.
Glare at the shinning twilight,
Let the breeze take you closer
To where you have chosen not to pass.

For a meaningful life
Is made up experiencing
These magical moments,
Rather than cautiously observing them
From behind a protective glass.

S.I.S

'The reason for this occurrence was written in the stars. It is destiny unfolding.'

When I Visit

Wonder if you feel my presence—
Near you, next to you, in you …
Wonder if you feel our essence—
On you, with you, through you …

J.V.D

'This life is nothing if it can not be shared.'

Eternal Love

My love for you was always certain,
But the distance between us left me confused.

Standing in as a curtain,
Those obstacles
Never allowed us to be fully amused.

They've followed us for years,
They've haunted us for lifetimes.

So many lost tears.

So much lost time, suffering of every kind.

Love keeps bringing you back to me,
When separated by the vastest sea.
Let's put an end to the separation,
Let's live a life full of aspiration,
Let's seek final retribution,
Let's satisfy love
Through our eternal unification.

S.I.S

'Remove your lenses in order to see more clearly. If still in doubt, than ask the truth to be revealed to you in the form of a dream.'

Love's Maze

There are hidden floors
Beyond trap doors—

Be careful where you tread …

The great love maze
Instills a craze
On each and every head.

Go around the walls
Or break them down—

No need to frown …

The Center of Love
Beholds the dove—

Transcend above …

There are hidden floors
Beyond trap doors—

Be careful where you tread …

The great love maze
Instills a craze
On each and every head.

Do not become entangled.

J.V.D

'Dizziness hits when you become still.'

The Mermaid Bride

She looks at her reflection
And wonders why,
The ripples in the water
Don't reply.

Where are the answers
To the questions I present?

Please respond,
So you'll allow me to enjoy
The time here
Which I patiently spend.

The black mask I wear around my eyes, protects me
From all the lies.

But even I, the eternal loyal lover,
Must see the world for what it really can be—
Or else I'll have to retire to land,
And stop questioning the sea.

S.I.S

*'A cold heart can be thawed,
however be ready to donate heat with real
expectations of what you might get in return.'*

Perceptions

Whoever you want me to be, I will be—
I'm in everyone, and everyone is me.
See me in the woman, see me in the man;
See me inside of you, and take my left hand:

Marry not a fool, but the one you do love—
Because only then, will you transcend above.
So be careful, my dear, who you see in me—
Though I am all, it is you who sets us free.

J.V.D

'Turn on the radio.
The next full song you hear
will apply to your situation.'

True Representation

You sit with your back turned
As the candles flicker.

However I know where your eyes glare—
Right through my soul,
As we realized
Why our lives needed to be shared.

We worked and played,
Laughed and prayed ...
Celebrated,
And even at times, strayed.

I watched you grow in so many ways,
And God I am eternally proud
Of your deserved praise.

I was not only a temporary
Or false representation of what you thought—
Please accept that at times,
My reality would slip
Because of all the ways I was distraught.

All that doesn't matter now;
Even though I wish to part,
With leaving the truth in your hands ...

Because one day, we may find ourselves
On non judgmental and accepting lands.

Only a part of me is presented
In each of these scenes—
Now that the orders from above have passed,
And we've had to lift our screen.

But know that I will try my best
To always see when your eyes are closed—
In order to guide you—
In the best form,
Of life's music composed.

S.I.S

*Fear and doubt imprison you.
Assess your options and outcome
with a brave heart.'*

Cupid's Rhythm

The shutters on the window
Rattled in the moonlight's glow—
Gentle wind delivering
A message from Cupid's Bow ...

A whistling arrow flying,
Forewarning of a dying—
In a note pinned to the roof
Where the fiddler stood crying:

"Hear my song world," He said—
On his knees, bowing his head;
While inside the room below
A woman awoke in bed ...

Wondering about a dream,
Her eyes widened with a beam—
Staring into The Color
Present in her Blanket's Seam:

The simple threads intertwined
Reminded her All's Divine—
As then the shutters opened ...
Giving her another sign.
Suddenly she heard the song,
That the fiddler played so long—
So she followed the music,
To that which would make her strong

And on the roof there was change—
No fiddler—which might seem strange …
Only a note that read, "LOVE"—
Perfect aim from Cupid's Range.

J.V.D

'Manipulation is the worst form of terrorism.'

Blossoms

Have you ever seen flowers cheerless?

Sometimes angels use them as a way to bless.

So many colors, so many shades—
Their fragrance enraptures us and invades.

And in their magical state of delight,
Choose a rose, a lily or petunia
To ensure that your special day is bright.

S.I.S

'You are dying until you are Living.'

Jewels

You compare me to diamonds,
But you forget I break.

You describe me through rubies,
But once in a while, to my real emotions
You must awake.

I am able to shine,
Beyond even what you have seen.

The sparkle of my eye needs to be discovered
As you lift my protective screen.
Handle me with caution,
Sweet traveler of life—

For those who ignore this advice
Often realize the feather in their hand
Just might be a rather sharp knife.

S.I.S

'If you whole heartedly believe in something, whatever it may be, do not allow anyone to convince you otherwise. However, this freedom of thought comes with a responsibility of not trying to impose your belief onto others.'

Whispers

You are countless miles away,
But distance never stopped our love.
I have waited Eternities;
Both with and without you nearby—
To see you again, to kiss you;
And to whisper in your ear.

The seas between us know our plight.
They carry our love onto shores,
Motioning to mountains our names—
So that they may be etched in stone;
And seen, together, by we all,
No matter a person's place.

Vast lands filled with forests hear us;
Birds sing our song from tree to tree.

The winds hum each sweet melody
Until a butterfly comes near
And flutters my whispers to you,
Each moment we are apart.

J.V.D

*'Never underestimate your natural abilities. Pass
on a talent, kind action and/or smile today, and
feel it travel the world.'*

Wanderer

Been there time and time again—
Always wondered when he'd appear.

Like a deep poem written,
His beauty made me fear:

All that I'd lose by just one glance—

From those penetrating eyes,
Ready to take me to another place.

Was I ready for this chase?

Breathless
Anxious
Winded
Restless

Who is this wanderer?

He's looking at me with those eyes—
Don't think he realizes their power ...

How many others before me
Have felt paralyzed, hour after hour?

He never said a word,
Just smiled and stared—
Glided through me time and time again.
No way I could turn back now,
Even if he were to leave again …

Knowing I had tasted him;
Knowing I had been one with him—
For a second or eternity …

Will feel the same with this Wanderer:

Breathless
Anxious
Winded
Restless

He's unreachable, inaccessible,
Unattainable, impossible.

He's a wanderer,
Here to leave and back again.

Do I make it begin or let it end?

Intoxicated, mesmerized,
Am I flying through the skies?

Do I turn around and ignore his scent?
Can't believe I finally found him—
I don't think I could walk away …
His dance makes me high again;
His moves drive me insane with pain …

He knows I need him
Gotta touch and breathe him …

If only he would stay long enough,
I'd ask nothing more from him.

Breathless
Anxious
Winded
Restless

He's unreachable, inaccessible,
Unattainable, impossible.

He's a wanderer,
Here to leave and back again.
Do I make it begin or let it end?
Who is this beautiful wanderer?

Who is this beautiful Wanderer?

S.I.S

'Children often know better than we do.'

Divine Touch

You kiss me so softly,
With lips of honey …

But the purified taste of love,
The exchange of Rumi's passion,
Create a heavy impact.

I become still in a moment, unable to move.

Our spirits are caught dancing, flying—

And my body becomes weak
In your captivating presence.

My knees gently shudder to rise again,
But I remain, in between life and death—
Praying—
Praying for you.

You guide me back toward the ground,
Reminding me of the many duties we have

And I am abandoned through our union,
While taken away from the suffering—
The great and ongoing suffering
Of the world.

Your Golden Character sticks to my lips
And I can not deny you.

I can not forget the taste of eternity;
Nor the sweetness of life
And the presence of wings.

I will not.

The kiss we share follows me like a shadow—
A reflection, dwelling in the temple I Am …
It becomes the windows to my soul,
The focus in my eyes,
Forever changing perception.

And as I return to that which beckons me …
Am I to pass on this kiss …
Share it in the next breath …

Or does it still belong to you?

J.V.D

'Willingly Let Go.'

Where Are We Now?

Another day,
Another chance to pave the way
With golden bricks, silver feathers
And magic sticks.

The Queen seldom awoke
With doubt or fright.
Why, when one can be consumed by excite, delight and a
Powerful light?

But this day all that was pure and exciting seemed
To have left her side.
Delight and excite had traveled
To a far off great divide.

Who could blame these two important companions for wanting
To escape to other situations?
Had they been nurtured and respected by their host?
Are they not like limbs amputated when ignored and
Unexplored?

The Queen had done all she could to illicit positive feelings
And inspiration.
But she did not exist alone
And therefore needed to live amongst other different creations.

Most of them did not share in her passion.
Most of them followed the same fashion.
Most of them wouldn't dare innovate.

Most of them only knew one way,
And that was to imitate.

'This day will be different,' thought the Queen.
'I will not accept the same old answers from my council.'

'Oh please, God of love and mercy,
I beg you to invite a soul that is enlightened,
Enchanted and free of screens.'

The Persian Queen conducted her assembly
With usual nobility and respect,
Allowing silence to invite all thinkers
To step forth and resurrect.
The ideas discussed and presented
Were significantly important and necessary—
Just alright, but nowhere near powerful enough
To once again invite back our two friends—
Do you remember who they are?

Ahh yes, delight and excite.

Her Highness slowly scanned the room for the chosen one.
She knew he was there, but not wanting to disrespect
Or hurt none.
He deserved a golden invitation,
A few glances—perhaps words of private exaltation.

The poet remained silent,
Standing reflectively in the far corner of the room throughout.

Never once seeming anything less than devout
To the kingdom that had offered him life—wealth—
But at times made him suffer from emotional drought.

He knew timing was everything and that there was a fine line
Between being eager and showing irritation.

His Persian Queen would soon beckon him
To speak of the Kingdom of Dreams
On the golden stage of respect and recognition.

The Queen and Poet had always a silent language.
They were able to communicate with a sigh, a blink of an eye—
As both eagerly waited for an often profound reply.

The invitation came in the form of a gracious nod.
The Queen weaved toward the Poet each thread
Of the welcoming red carpet, as she glanced his way
And made sure
No one would think him to be odd.

'I have heard from most of my loyal subjects
About where we are now—
However our poet has not shared with us,
What he thinks and how.'
He hesitated for a fraction of an instant,
Not for any other reason than knowing
Precisely the sometimes shallow understanding of his people.
'Your Majesty, to me, a Poet,
I would say we are in the Kingdom of Dreams—
A Kingdom where I am your King and you are my Queen.

The Poet suddenly grew in the eyes of his Queen.
She stared up at him as if she were in awe of the most
Breathtaking steeple.

He continued dancing with words that made her fly.
She became the trees, the birds and butterflies that he stood by,
Intoxicating her, making her feel high.

But he was not only on that golden stage to impress her.

For that, he knew she had many.
It was his purpose on that hour,
And for years to come
To wake her up to epiphanies.

'Your answer to the question my Grace can only be truthfully
Answered by another question.'

'And what question is that?' Asked the Queen

'It is the same question that is the lock to heavens key, it is the
Question of where do you choose to be?'

With those magical words, delight and excite
Immediately returned
To the right and left side of the ruler.
No one else could have brought them back to her majesty—
With such force—
Not the jester, the judge or even the jeweler!

The others, first worried
Soon felt the ripple effect of the poet's words.
They watched the Queen's smile
And decided they wanted to eternally be
Part of this Sheppard's herd.
'Let me answer your question wise Poet, if you shall allow me.
For it is through such deep exchanges that you and
I often discover
Many vast new seas.
I thank you for reminding me once again about
The word 'choice'.
It is through this powerful tool that most of us have
Been given a voice
To reach those less 'choiceful' than our selves,
Those unfortunate enough to have placed their dusted
And withered souls
On useless and empty shelves.'

'Thank you Poet
For posing this important question,
Not just to me—
But to all those needing a reminder
And direction.
Those evil forces you spoke about
May even ponder over such an idea
By 'choosing' to be a brave knight
Rather than an evil sorcerer
On a cold Eastern night.'

'Now dear Poet know that you can rest at ease not because you
Have left your Queen incredibly pleased
But more importantly you have ceased to simply be a devotee.
You have also released an infectious philosophy into our world
For all who wish to be insane with sanity and not just idle
Humanity.'

'I knew your kind existed in our kingdom,
No matter how different or rebellious.
Believe in your species our Poet,
For it is far more adventurous.
You hesitated to speak today—
But please,
Never allow hesitation
To hold you back again.
Like golden rain,
Cover us with your words
That long to be the whispering campaign
For all those listening,
Waiting on this incredible
And sometimes rough terrain.'

'But you know dear Poet
What makes me most happy
About our exchange here today?
It is that you are where you want be
And that is absolutely blissful to me.'

S.I.S

'Think carefully why you desire something so deeply. If the intentions are not pure, the universe may decide otherwise for you.'

In the Kingdom of Dreams

Words escaped the Poet's page and fluttered with butterflies. Free-floating through marmalade skies, they sang with birds—to be heard by shooting stars and echoed beneath cascading waterfalls. Like Prometheus' numbers, they could be added, subtracted, multiplied, divided, repeated, attributed and simplified in a myriad of patterns—formulating rare and eternal languages, only to be recognized by those with beautiful eyes. Blind men could see them; deaf men could hear them; crippled men walked with them ... But jesters sometimes juggled them; magic sometimes manipulated them and too often, precious patterns were ignored and unexplored, misinterpreted and misunderstood.

Always with an open door, the Poet befriended words most. When nonsensical chatter visited, however, he found himself more comfortable in the company of silence.

The Poet perpetually sought to teach new ways of seeing, new ways of hearing, new ways of interpreting, new ways of tasting, new ways of feeling—to any persons near him—but repeatedly, the people were not willing to listen or to learn. Thus through his continuous endeavors, the Poet internalized infinite lessons with each waking moment and his appreciation for life grew—however with an unsettling loneliness.

The more knowledge he obtained, the more wisdom he realized; the more he tried to turn darkness into light, paper into trees, and the shackles people chose to hold onto, into golden goblets filled with pure waters from the ocean of truth.

The Poet's alchemy was magnificently enchanting, but because the people would not listen, they remained enslaved. The Poet then tried methods to reduce their pain and release their burdens—but too many times, the Poet was left with no energy, only carrying things that were not his.

How could this be? Upon waking each morning the poet prayed to the sun, and in the evening, he spoke to the moon. With every new day came renewed energy and aspirations, but soon the Poet realized, to fulfill his quest, he would have to stop carrying unnecessary weight altogether.

If it were only him, the Poet felt he had everything in the world he needed, but nobody to share it with. He knew others like himself existed but he had yet to meet the soul he had longed for.

Sometimes he had dreams of her. Sometimes, when he closed his eyes he could feel his soul escape his body and fly around worlds of infinite possibilities, holding her hand, inapprehensive of any uncertainty.

He could feel her mesmerizing presence wherever he was though he had not yet met her outside of his dreams—or so he had once thought.

But when blue flames in the background of starlight passionately flickered in her eyes, he decided to once again listen to the signs, to believe in the life, to believe in himself.

One morning the Poet awoke to an invigorating feeling and when he opened his window wide, with his head out toward the sunrise as usual, two birds came to his side, nodding toward the palace, and whispered, "She is the One." The Poet was stunned, unsure how to interpret the message.

"Who better to guide you about your visions than the Queen of the Kingdom of Dreams," continued one of the birds.

The Poet thanked the birds and together the three of them sang in song to bless the day. The birds flew off and dancing with his feet, the Poet followed his own rhythmic beat. Perhaps the birds knew something he did not, he thought—perhaps they have only told him what he needed to know to get his feet moving.

"Where will this path I choose to follow lead me?" wondered the Poet.

As he pondered his query, he remembered that sometimes answers lie within the questions themselves.

"If I choose to follow this path," said the Poet, "this path will lead me to where I choose to be."

The Poet embarked on a journey toward the Queen.

Although the palace stood atop an enormous mountain, he was not in the least discouraged. He believed there was always a way. The Poet passed through thick forests full of wandering colors and dazzling figures. He fed himself berries of red and purple and blue, and seized shelter in the trunks of trees. There, in the trunks of trees he would shield himself from the cold winds that sometimes caused him to stumble due to their swift force.

The Poet never minded the cold, as long as warmth resulted. The Poet believed that everything was intertwined and when it snowed, he liked to think each glistening snow flake had fallen from an angel's wing.

When it rained, he heard melodies of life—if he wanted, he could hear the moonlight sonata in accordance with each drop—imagining piano keys being played with each refreshing splash.

Each time an autumn leaf fell, he was reminded of new beginnings, and when the summer sun irresistibly bathed him in warmth, he always bathed himself in cool waters beyond crystal white beaches.

Twenty-two days had passed before the Poet reached the bottom of the mountain and by then he had not had a plan to reach the top—but he knew, through his multiple journeys, he had had the abilities. He could climb but there was not enough time.

The Poet knew the Queen was extremely busy and did not want to make assumptions about her own role and circumstances as what the birds told him was too abstract.

He could ask the Queen to come out and see him, but first he would have to establish a forum of communication—this could not be easily done as he had not yet met the Queen!

The Poet decided to start climbing a tree near the mountain. When he reached a far branch, he swung from it and just managed to leap onto a balanced ledge of stone. There was still a long way to go. The Poet would not give up.

With his head toward the stars, the Poet was reminded of infinite possibilities. On the twenty-forth day, in the distance, he saw what appeared to be the brightest star he had ever laid eyes upon. As it seemingly floated toward him, the Poet grew curious as to whether or not this amazing light was indeed a star or something else against all odds.

The glowing image continued to swiftly glide through the sky, and the Poet began to sing a song—similar to the one he sang every morning with the birds.

Upon hearing this harmonious voice, the enigmatic source of life came close to the Poet. The Poet was zealously surprised, as the seemingly star was a living creature—a beautiful winged horse named Pegasus—often spoke about in myths but rarely seen. The Poet remained in awe. Immediately he wondered if Pegasus would help him. He explained to the enchanting creature about his journey toward the Queen, along with all the incredible experiences he had had along the way. Now he needed to reach the palace.

Without the Poet having to say anything more, Pegasus looked him directly in his eyes and asked if he was willing to take a ride. Together they soared through the skies—weaving in and out of clouds, catching falling stars and journeying toward the Queen. With his gleaming, extensive wings, the marvelous horse of melody and magic led the Poet to the palace he had been searching for. Little did the Poet know, that there, not only would he find the Queen, but he would also meet an extremely familiar face.

The Queen was in her garden. She planted seeds of wisdom and watched life sprout out from the grounds beneath her. Although the Poet increasingly felt the presence of someone familiar nearby, he was still afar and had not yet seen this beautiful picture. The Queen was always up for a dance and decided to listen to some music. As she had left the garden to go to her ballroom, the Poet had meanwhile stumbled upon the magical array of flowers.

The garden was extraordinary, and in the centre was planted a white rose. The Poet knew he was on a mission to find the Queen, but he always permitted with life to make time to appreciate.

He leaned over to speak to the rose, and upon touching its petal, the white burst into yellow and then red, and so on to millions of interchanging colors. The Poet felt the beauty of the moment in motion, and the Flower said to him, "Listen to the song."

Again, the Poet was astounded.

He all of a sudden heard the most striking sound upon his ears. A rhythm like no other—the same rhythm he sang every morning. Never had he heard the sound generate from anywhere else but the birds and butterflies—but at this moment he heard a human voice which was not his own.

He followed the notes into the palace, into the library, in and out of multiple rooms, until finally; he stood in front of two golden doors which reached the ceiling of the palace's height. The doors were open. Inside, he saw the most gorgeous woman dancing to the tune of life, singing with the sounds, eyes closed and moving so graciously he had thought he spotted an angel in the flesh. Upon a closer glance he realized that the woman before him, the Queen, was also the woman in his dreams.

The Poet entered the room and said not a word. He gently walked toward the Queen and took her hand to join her in dance. Gladly she took his hand and without having to open her eyes she knew that her chosen one had stood before her. The Poet closed his eyes and accompanied the Queen on an exquisite expedition. Their feet moved in syncopation and they danced together as one until the floor spun for itself and swirls circled in patterns beneath their shoes.

When they opened their eyes, they were tap-dancing on rainbows and soon lying in a green field surrounded by candy dandelions and purple orchids. Nearby a clear blue river sparkled with pebbles of sweet honey-glazed almonds and chamomile Lillie pads.

Encircled by this enchantment, the Queen and the Poet watched the sun set before their vision and basked beneath the stars. When their eyes had finally met, they were immersed into one another's souls.

Subtly blowing into the Queen's ear, the Poet whispered three words, slowly and powerfully:

"Dare to Imagine."

The words gravitated toward the Queen's heart and in a suddenly swift moment, the Queen felt them inside her—like jazz jumping in her stomach and rumbling in her mind—until each word burst through every limb of her body like warm lightening striking from the sky unto her and into the ground.

The single moment held within itself infinite lives, experiences, beginnings, memories—all of which words could not nearly depict. Then, as if they had rehearsed it, at the exact same time, both the Queen and the Poet looked at one another and whispered, "Let us go there again—that is where I want to be …"

"With you," continued the Poet.

Together, the Queen and the Poet embraced the love of silence. Afterward they thanked the birds, the sun and moon, and went on singing their song to bless the day.

J.V.D

'Each string in a guitar serves its role in fulfilling a chord—just as every tapped place on a drum gives vibration to a unique sound (differing with speed, force and the hand which embraced it). We are all instruments of the DIVINE. Our HEARTS are harps played by angels, and when UNITED TOGETHER, song manifests into dance—gently whirling through souls, universes and new experiences—rising like the Sun, both above and below an infinite horizon.'

'Shhhhh ...

Do you see me?
Always.

Do you love me?
For ever and a few days.
When will it ever end?
When a circle ends.
Was I wrong?
Only those times
When you were sure you were right.
Are there others?
Some have already found you.
Who shall I learn from?
Those learning from you.

Who are you?
You.

S.I.S

Love Is Inescapable'

Wherever we find ourselves,
It shall be felt—
And so shall it be celebrated.
Should you ever feel lost, or in darkness,
Let love guide you home;
And should you ever feel unappreciated
Or misunderstood, in any circumstance,
Let love remind you—that you, and I, that WE,
Are the purest truth, the purest love—
Beyond right and wrong, good and bad.
And when you find that eternal bliss is within,
Love shall also be felt dancing within.
And when you smile unto all that surrounds you—
From mountains and stars, to trees and seeds,
In a garden forever blossoming,
You shall be smiling with love—
For just as our love eternally cherishes you,
You shall forever remember, feel and learn from
The essence here, within and beyond …
… YOU ARE LOVE;
… A love with divine wings
That shall flutter beyond humankind,
Into the eternal heavens visited in dreams,
Beckoning us to enter
Now,
In this moment.

J.V.D

Serendipitous ...

You
Own
Unconditionally
So much ...
of my Emotion ...
Forever

S.I.S

About the Authors

Shaheem and Delalunas are more than authoring poets—they are the loving light reflected in all their words, and the soulful essence connecting human platforms to spiritual horizons.

Uniquely differentiated by their sense of style and refined approaches, Shaheem and Delalunas successfully weave together dreams, experiences and unexplored realities into page-turning adventures; filled with philosophic and esoteric expeditions of magic, mystery and the seemingly mundane. Through their works, they reintroduce the infinite potential of our true being and redefine social norms; striving to awaken a greater conscious-ness—in readers, and in humanity.

As founders of the Peace*Metamorphasis on Frequency™ campaign, Shaheem and Delalunas encourage all people to follow their creative passions, and inspire us (both as individuals and as a whole), to recognize our roles, choices and abilities, in the book we call Life.

Samineh Izedi Shaheem is author of the novel, *The Karma Hotel*; and is also one of the featured writers of *All Women Magazine*, a publication distributed throughout the Middle East. She has a very unique monthly column focusing on the diverse cultural character of the region: readers write in their issues/concerns and she tries to the best of her ability to guide them in the right direction. Samineh is also an assistant professor of Psychology at the American International University in London. She takes her role to educate very seriously, and aims to reach as many individuals who may require guidance during the trying stages of their educational period, as well as throughout life, in order to make a difference. Samineh is Canadian, but from a Middle Eastern background (Iranian); and has studied and worked in different parts of the world, including The United Sates of America, The Netherlands, The United Arab Emirates, and of course, London.

Jacquelyn (JV) Delalunas is author of the novels, ***Children of the Sky*** and ***Memories on a Tree***. As a universal advocate for the realization of One Consciousness—worldwide and beyond—Jacquelyn's books are well known for strategically sharing passages in developed and distinct ways, previously unseen and unrecorded in today's book industry. By highlighting inner stories and natural rhythms through in-text color psychology, applied with each novel's content and aesthetic, Jacquelyn reveals a deeper story line and puzzle, contained within each creation (an innovative method never before explored in 'fictional' print). Rather through multifaceted poetry or her signature literary technique, Jacquelyn's instinctive craft, consistently invites readers to new levels of thinking, and new ways of life. Both the context and natural character of her work re-spark ardent vitality in everyday occurrences, and beckon us inside doors of infinite existence. While most of Jacquelyn's creations cross-market standard literary genres, all words by JV Delalunas can, in one way or another, best be described as Magical Realism. For more information, please visit: *www.delalunas.com*

978-0-595-48209-2
0-595-48209-0

Printed in the United Kingdom
by Lightning Source UK Ltd.
126858UK00001B/343-345/P

The Gift of Sirr